covered in vibrant color

poetry & affirmations
by
brynnen beierle

illustrations
by
juju bradley

covered in vibrant color is a collection of poetry and prose diving through the ins and outs of mental health, as well as the ups and downs of our chaotic lives. it is divided into two phases: the broken and the bloomed. first, you are taken through the broken (the heartache, depression, and pain), and then it transitions into the bloom (the forgiveness, love, and self-discovery) to really share the journey that constitutes my whirlwind of emotions. ultimately, i hope this book allows you to feel less alone and remain hopeful when you're feeling broken, and it encourages you to embrace your bloom when you feel whole.

welcome to my vibrant soul.

PHASE 1
the broken

seasonal

i lost my name
in the absence of sobriety

i've misplaced a lot since then
like who i am
and where i've been

i'm a little lost in my head i think
but the whiskey seems to help
and there isn't much else to do
when my old friend creeps back in

she used to come only seasonally
but i think she's been here for quite some time now
making a home of me
and burying me
in her vibrancy

she's never welcome
but she never leaves
even when i ask
that she let me be

but that's another thing i've lost
a voice of my own

lack of sobriety
seems to take a lot from me.

bottom of the well

i want to stay
in this pit of nothingness –
the depths that bury themselves so deep
that even the pain is numbed

please just leave me here,
i promise to come back when i'm ready.

damned and the dying

you drained the light in me
the way autumn does to leaves

a slow,
beautiful
tragedy.

lack of love

i guess i finally lost all hope
in who i thought you were
and who we could be

with that dream stripped from me
i feel a little lost
and a little empty

i could've held my grip forever
had you just let me

but i guess you'll stay in my mind
forever
as what we could've been

but never will be.

boston

i wanna run
to a place where no one knows my name
i don't know who i am anymore anyway
and people here destroyed too much of me

i need a new sunset
a bigger place to explore
just a place i can regroup
where my heart can be restored

i wanna run
to where they don't know about the pain
i don't know what happened to the former me anyway
and people here drenched me in shades darker than ever before.

draining

i became the water that fed you
but you expected me to be the sun too

i ended up completely draining myself
because you hoped to find the missing light in me
and not in you.

x

false hope

be careful believing
in who others could be

a faith like that
can leave you buried in devastation

it's like watering a plant
that gets no sun;
you will provide the water
but you'll be draining yourself
when they choose to dim the light within.

hope, less

your kindness,
it struck me.
i had never been so cared for,
never loved so tenderly.
it began to grow a hope in me
that i had never believed in before
a hope i truly didn't know was even there,
until it forcefully vanished from my grip.
---
that's the thing about hope, though,
you don't realize it's been embedded in you
until it's gone,
pulled away like the ground beneath your feet,
leaving you lost and off balance
and you're just left hearing another "i'm sorry"

as if "sorry" could ever restore
the hole of empty faith
that has now been placed
in your hopeless heart.

remembering you

remembering you
comes with feelings,
not thoughts

it comes with feelings of anxiety
pain
and regret

feelings of confusion
devastation
and love.

your smile holds emotions
that i thought i had buried.

chaos

it's everywhere i go
it's in everyone i meet
but the thing is,
is they weren't that way before me

it's not on my face
it's buried beneath
but i can't fix it now
the scars are too deep

i am the chaos.

the pain

it was not permanent
and it was not constant
but it did linger
and it came crashing down in waves
that were unexpected
and violent

leaving me gasping for air
and wandering aimlessly
in a newly shaded
darker
existence.

giving

i've learned that giving is a bad thing

not of gifts
not of honesty
not even of love —

but the giving of yourself
your deepest truths
your vulnerability

when somebody knows you,
knows your soul,
they can never unknow

they will obtain words that can cut deeper,
hurt more

and when they leave,
those parts of you can never be restored.

nothingness

irrelevant
nothingness

i feel nothing other than irrelevancy
and nothing other than that

the immovable empty space
that seems to be taking up
all of my being

"my being"
that is nothing
other than a floating,
implacable object

absolute
nothingness.

the vibrance of you

you planted this seed of sadness in me
and life waters it
in the randomest of things

like going to the grocery store and seeing the peanut butter i used to buy,
but i no longer do because it was for you

or the songs that came on when i left your house
for the very last time

each one of these moments,

the sadness blooms

and it grows inside of me

in all the ways i was wrapped

and consumed in you.

and this seed is rooted in me
and it's caused me to turn away
from all of my favorite things
as they're somehow embedded in you

so

i hate coffee
i hate my favorite band
i hate going to the movies
and i hate all my plants
(which really sucks because we both know how much i loved those)
but the sight of them takes me back to your room
when the sun peaked through your window
and reflected off the one in your windowsill
and i never knew that would be something i missed about you

but i remember all of these parts of you
and us
and it has made me hate everything
so much

because everything now feeds this sadness
as long as it waters the thought of you.

evergreen

i can't let go of our love
because it was the evergreen kinda love

you know the kind

the kind that ends the way it started:
up in flames
setting souls on fire
failing only due to circumstance
with an everlasting desire.

rabbit hole

sometimes i'm forced to surrender
to the overbearing thoughts of you
it's almost as if
my mind enjoys being consumed
the way my heart used to.

void

i've discovered
the hard way
that life does go on
without you

but when your presence
makes an appearance in my mind
and i realize that you're only here
mentally
and still completely absent
physically

i still feel empty

spaces of me will always
feel vacant without you.

dr. depression

he came knocking on my door
with no motives other than his weekly routine
of demanding my freedom;
forcefully filling my sorrows
and completely draining my spirit.

broken fragment

nothing has been the same
since you left

i still have parts of me
but you ran off with the rest.

curiosity kills

curiosity kills a lot of things
but my innocence was not one of them

my innocence was ripped out of my hands
and covered in the bloody palms of yours
it was buried deep under your fingernails
leaving stains on your wrist as a branded glory

my curiosity fell victim to the selfishness of yours
and your broken, shaking hands,
took the full length of my imagination with them.

missing you

i don't know when i'll stop missing you
but i hope it's sometimes soon

because i don't wanna lose me
after already losing you.

flames

i burnt all our memories away –
i couldn't just toss them
i needed them in flames
not to forget you
but to forget the pain

you left me here
so damaged and broken –
leaving in a rush
with my final words left unspoken

i'm so lost now.
i'm just falling apart
looking for something
-anything-
to unbreak my stupid heart

i burnt all our memories away –
i couldn't just toss them
i needed them in flames.
to forget you too
because you said you'd stay.

stored

the thing is
when i hurt
the pain does not feel new

it feels more so
that it has been reopened

like it's a dark place in my soul
under a jurisdiction still unknown

and when it decides to open
-under an authority that seems to not be my own-

it opens abruptly,
aggressively,
and consumingly

a thick darkness is released,
it completely surrounds me

it flows from within me

this pain does not feel new.

rain

the sound of rain
reminds me of you
because rain reminds me of home
and home is drenched in you.

gone

you stole my heart —
you completely ran away with it

but then you left

you never brought it back.

conclusion

i live in a world
too cruel for a love like mine.

everywhere

the worst part about you leaving
is that you're not even gone

you are still everywhere —
every song I hear
every book I read
every movie I watch —
your laugh bursts in my soul
the way your love still runs through my veins.

can't you just let me be?
can't this pain just leave
so that i can be free?
but you took so much from me,
you see,
that now i'm not sure
if i'll ever be
fully me.

consumed

the dark clouds devoured me
they soaked up every ounce
of light i had

instead of any form of sun
my veins raced with vibrant black.

when i wake up, keep the lights off

self-care

they say that's what i'm lacking

but i showered today
and i brushed my hair
and i flossed my teeth
and i put on real pants
and i drank two water bottles

i recycled them too

what they don't understand is
some days that *is* self-care for me —
actually making it out of bed
and turning the lights on
and looking in the mirror
without wanting to cry

it's just that

the presence of my depression
strips the life from me
the way shades do to a room
and i have to beg my mother
to let me be
because i tried to get up
but i couldn't

and as she leaves
she'll keep the door cracked

and hey, mom,
when i wake up

keep the lights off this time
i'll turn them on
when the sun breaks.

solo

i stopped believing in love long ago
i learned the only thing i can truly believe in is me

but i'm not just calling out love's bluff;
i don't believe in friendship either

i believe in one thing,
i believe in me.

franklin

you're still buried in the scars

the scars from the anxiety
the anxiety that led to acne
and the acne that led
to deeply rooted scars
on my permanently rosie cheeks

you're in every scar
and i think of you
every time i see my own face

and if you look close enough
the scars even spell out your name.

stay, please

i know i do this
i know i take you down with me
and rattle your emotions
the same way mine are bouncing
inside of my own head
i know i make you worry
and irritate you with distress and chaos

i know i should be stronger
i know i shouldn't need you here
but i'm begging you this time

please don't go
before i get better.

it's okay / loving addict p.1

and "it's okay"
i'll say

add it in,
toss it on,
add more to this baggage
you've built upon my shoulder blades

and it's okay
have another drink while you're at it
sip it down,
toss it back,
add more to this buzz
you've built your life around

and it's okay
give your grief to me too
make sure that my own feelings
have absolutely no room

and it's okay
you can leave your stains of regret
on the floor
i'll clean them up in the morning
with the mess you made of me, too

and it's okay
i'll be okay
steady hoping
that you will be too.

life without you

it's been one whole year
so why does it still feel
like it was yesterday?

why do i still feel
like i can't live without you?

why do i feel like i lost you
so recently?

my soul misses you.

i wish you would've stayed.

depression waves

it's a rollercoaster
this depression of mine

an endless up and down
of light and sorrow
nausea and sunlight

sometimes i can't breathe
and the oxygen is stripped from my lungs

but some days
i want to live forever
in the freeness
of being happy
being still
and being alive

and i guess you can cast your votes in the morning
on whether or not
i'll be coasting
or crashing.

the love won't fade

i can't get you off my mind
you are absolutely embedded
every vein, every thread
drenched in words
i wish
you'd never said.

the thickness of pain

experiencing pain is one thing
becoming it is another

when the pain is ripping at your skin
bursting through your veins,
begging to come out,
you eventually surrender

and the pain is no longer a feeling
the pain is you

light is no longer visible,
your body: no longer tangible
hope: not even fathomable

all you see, feel, and know
all that you are
is dark, vibrant pain.

footprints

i took the long way out
but i left deep footprints
hoping that if you wanted
you could find them
and follow me

knowing
though
that they would eventually be washed out
over time by the rain

and there will be no trace of me anymore
or us
and we'll slowly drip
down the drain
along with the last of my footprints
to you.

flying

the weight of our souls connection
was heavier than expected
i grew far too fond of the joy
and the wings i grew with you
---
i think you'll always be a part of me
but it's killing me to know —
is it the same for you?
or am i holding onto a love
that is long gone?
a love that doesn't believe
the way that i do;
a love that flies further on without me
as i glide behind
in the midnight sky.

happy holidays

but it runs in the family
so maybe i'll give it a shot

or two

until my knees fall to the floor
and my head is in the toilet
and i'm pouring out
years worth
of built up pain
to my poor baby sister
who has now replaced me
as the chaotic family's care-taker,

holding hair back on holidays
instead of high hopes

but it'll just be this one time
and hell
i deserve a break right?
i earned a little let-loose
and it won't hurt my sister
if it's just this once
she'll understand when she's older
the same way that i did
that this is the only way to survive
the holidays in the family
and that's why mom does it too
so it'll all be fine

until it's not
and my sisters last in line
and we've all wasted away
drowning our heads
in tangled vines and vodka drops.

utah

covered in pain
covered in you
drenched in dark shades
accompanying me in my room

my heart felt hollow
my mind felt weak
the thought of you,
i could not speak

i will never go back
because i'd relive the cold,
the pain that cut me
too deep in my soul.

prints of darkness / loving an addict p.2

the trigger is always the same
but the pain prints differently

last time i was shattered
i cried as i picked up
the broken pieces of my heart
on the floor

the print was red that day

the time before that
i lived in yellow bliss
i was giving up that time
on you
i was sure
your addiction wouldn't
shade me too

i wore yellow prints of relief that day

the time in between those
my god
it was black
i was drowning in anger
disappointment
loneliness
i didn't think i'd come back
from that one
but you did
so i did too

black is the one that comes back

but this time
the trigger
printed out in blue

blue with hope
love
and forgiveness

please get better this time
so we can stay
living
in this blue

if you don't
we won't
and i won't stay
to live another black.

can't contain it if it's not tangible

depression waves crash in like the sun
but with the absence of light

it is uncontrollable
vibrant
and cannot be contained

the swell pulls me under
and the waves crash into me

i can't slow it down, move it,
or escape it.

they (waves)

they race
they crash
they break
they last

they come and go
far too fast.

but you planted first

you didn't know who you were
and i found you there

i watched you unravel
and discover yourself
in untouched depths

i watered you
as you blossomed
and grew completely
tangled in me

and maybe that's why it ripped me in two
when you left
because we grew together
and my roots were embedded in yours

until one day
you decided to plant elsewhere
and grow further
without these roots of mine
tying you down.

no place like not being home

"she's my little gypsy"
they say

"she's my wild soul"
they say

i am not your anything

i became this free spirit
because i wasn't your anything
you never gave me a home
so i left to make one of my own

and that gives you no right
to brag when i visit
acting as if you had any sort of
positive influence to the person i have become

i am not your anything.

grip

but how
just how
do i learn to loosen my grip
on something in which
i've held so tightly

how do i let go of the love we've built?

the love you so confidently told me
wouldn't go.

summertime sadness

summertime sadness —

wouldn't have come
if we would've lasted.

broken and unfair

what a mess of a man you are
breaking hearts because you don't know
what yours wants.

lack of worth

it's all downhill
when the doubt creeps in

when it makes its way
into your core and makes its living
off of the light in you

when the life is detoxed
out of you
and you're left searching
for any part
that may be left of you.

i'll miss you forever

i don't want to wake up
in my lights
if they no longer shine
in your life.

a shade lighter

it's effortless
this process of losing you
and i'm not quite sure
what to do

i don't think i know
how to be me
without a splash of you.

if we go down, we'll go down together

i'll be destruction
and you'll be my daylight
we'll dance and we'll tumble
until neither of us makes it out alive.

ticheville

i poured my heart out
to the riverbed
so i could watch my thoughts drown
the way my heart had.

unfair

i hate that you gave up on me
but i hate even more
that i can't give up on you

and what i hate the very most
is that
you don't care whether or not
i do.

wine stains

there's wine stains
slipping through the pages of my journal
as it drips from my lips

there seems to be an urge
to fight my sobriety
when the thought of you
sparks in me.

whatever's left

you left
and i was there
completely adrift

now i'm here searching
for whatever's left of me.

anxiety's goodbye's

i've become too good
at goodbyes i think

i had a lot of practice
on my father
you know

and it made my skin
tough to break

i don't even bleed
and my eyes can't cry

the goodbye comes naturally
and i won't even miss you
and it'll be my go-to
and i probably won't fight for you
because goodbyes are logical
and staying will be a mistake

and if you change your mind
and you try to stay
i'll be waiting
secretly
every day
for you to change your mind

so i'll cave
and i'll say goodbye first

giving you no choice
but to leave me behind.

pressure

and i can feel the weight on my shoulders
pressing down with every ounce of its being
fighting gravity
and making me smaller

it comes from you too
you know
all the pressures
and doubts
and loneliness
and fear

it's from the forgiveness that was forced upon me
the cheating i didn't deserve
the crushed dreams
the judgement
the somehow
overbearingly powerful ability
to make me question myself
and the worth i bring
the pressure to do more
be better
find happiness
love harder

it's exhausting me
and i can feel it
ripping a mess of me

because here's the truth
i want to just be
i refuse to fall in line with the hearts of despair
the one's that only flaw
is that they love too hard
leaving them with the biggest wounds
lying half alive with their backs on the floor

the ones that are trapped

wanting more and more and more
and more

i want to exist in where i'm at
not where i should be
or where we used to be

i need this weight stripped from me.

that half-ass love

i used to wholeheartedly admire
the love that you give
until i realized how unhealthy
and needed it was

i realized you'd love absolutely anyone
that showed they were capable
of loving you back
or even just touched you enough
until they pulled the heart off your sleeve

but i guess like all love
it taught me something

that i would rather not love at all
than love impurely
the way you loved
both me
and her.

friends can break your heart too

we were warned to draw a line
but we didn't
did we?

but i would've drawn it
and gone over it twice
with sharpie
had i known
that the lack thereof
would take you from me
so abruptly.

if trees could talk

if these trees could talk
they would tell the story of my soul
they would pour out every doubt and sorrow
my heart has contained

if these trees could talk
they would confess that i still love you
they would not be too proud
to tell you
that i still need you

but maybe

if these trees could talk
you'd be here
and i wouldn't be longing for you.

selfish habits

why do my bones crack
at the thought of you

how did i become this way?

i guess that's what happens
when men like you
give love
then take it away.

depression games

the vast emotions
you paint me in
change daily
and violently

i can't truly capture
how exhausting it is

and if we're being honest
i hate what you do to me
and i didn't even ask
for you to be a part of me.

not over you

some days i think i'm over you
most days, to be honest

but then i hear your name
or i see something that reminds me of you
and i catch myself picturing your vibrant smile
in a moment that's buried in our past

and i realize that i'm not
and i probably never will be

because i can't hear your name
without it sparking a flame.

dear you,

life is empty now.

- lonely

art and her flowers

why am i most inspired to write
when i'm heartbroken?

isn't the joy enough, too?

PHASE 2
the bloomed

morose - vibrant sun

i remember feeling lost
feeling morose
feeling like my head was under water
but without the sand in my toes.

the pain ran so deep then
i didn't think i'd make it.
i thought i was gonna die there
i could no longer take it.

---

it's been months now
and here i stand
having only a vague memory of the pain
as if this was all god's plan.

---

i remember feeling hope
feeling renewed
feeling like i could breathe again
and with a clearer view

the pain taught me something
that my faith lives in me,

-oh dear-

not in you.

resilient

when the pain runs too deep
when it races through your veins and nearly cracks your bones
when it holds so heavily in your heart that it frightens you to dive in fully,
breathe.
remember that you don't have to dive in
to the point of consumption
your pain can settle first
your heart can take a break from either having to love fully
or be filled with pain and resentment
your heart, like you, love, can just be.
---
and when you are ready
you can face your demons
you can tell them that you're stronger than they are
that though this pain exists,
you and your vibrant soul exist too.
that forgiveness lives in your heart,
and it strives deeper than this pain
that love still lives within you
and you will show yourself the immense compassion that your soul de-
serves.

even the deepest of all pain
cannot destroy a heart like yours.

defined

who you've been
what you've been through
and how you've been treated before
does not define you —
you are whoever you want to be
and you shine as bright as ever.

again

hi there
it's me again
and i know you're trying
to lock me out again
but i am here
and you know i'll win again
i'll rip through your skin
and leave you dry again

but that's how we work
we'll do this again
and again

i'll knock on your door
you'll let me in again
i won't just come
i'll become you again
we'll dance
we'll tumble
and we'll drown again

but that's how you work
you'll learn to swim again
and again

you'll catch your breath
and come back to shore again
you'll kick me out
and become the sun again
no matter how often you drown
you'll come up for air again

until one day
you'll never see me again.

growing up

the sun is setting
the sky is pink
i am in awe
she is at peace
i need a photo
she jumps from her knees
i am on my phone
she is soaring free
i'm lost thinking
of where else i could be
she is steady singing
dancing beneath the trees
i'm plotting my post
and who else will see
she is captivated
by the reflection of the sea
she is growing up,
she can't wait to be me

oh but what i would give to be her
and relive the magical age of three.

lost the battle

but we both fought as hard as we could
we held on so desperately,
maybe stronger than we should

but we couldn't loosen our grip
we wrapped our hands so tightly
to every last strand, every last strip

but slowly we slid,
further and further down this rope
gripping until our hands bled
holding onto every bit of hope

but we lost the war
and we're finally letting go
so here are my last words
that i think you should know:

i love you wholeheartedly
i believe in you so
i will miss your smile
and your vibrant soul as it glows
i will admire you from afar
and happily watch you grow

but truth be told,
i didn't want you to go.

advice

but if i could only tell you
in a way that you'd understand
that one day this will all be over –
it will be part of the past
that no matter how good a moment –
it will not last
remember that during the hard times
that this too shall pass

the hard times may feel longer
though
they don't go by as fast
but pain is only temporary

and you are who you are

don't let this cruel world
make you hide behind a mask.

incredible

your love moved me
because it taught me,
for the first time,
that something
doesn't need to be near the existence
of the mundane
to be viewed as extraordinary
sometimes it is just that:
absolutely and undoubtedly magnificent.

moving forward

i pictured myself peeling off my pain
my resentment
my guilt
my sorrows
and my self-limiting beliefs

putting it all into a box,
taping it up,
dropping it off on the side of an abandoned road

and then walking away

shining differently than ever before.

home

it frightens me
how comfortable i am in the wilderness

being lost and alone

feels too much like home.

heal

i envisioned my mind draining out the immense pain that it had been storing,
and being re-filled with pure, vibrant compassion.
the color that stuck with me, and for some reason always has,
is sky blue.
the pain being extracted was a glowing, strong shade of dark red.
the compassion flowing back into me was a light, yet very bold, beautiful shade of blue.
---
i believe i heal like this — patiently emptying out the unwanted, consuming misery,
and delicately filling my soul back up with the love and understanding that is so clearly needed.

i'm yours

looking into your eyes,
your sun-splattered face,
my heart gives way to yours
the way mountain tops
do to sunrise.

free

sand between the pages
salt water in my hair
my thoughts coming to life
breathing in the ocean air.

letting you go

i don't know how to let you go.

the thought of having your name mean nothing to me
after all this time —
all the laughs
all the love
all of us,
terrifies me.

and for the last few months
hearing your name has brought nothing but pain
but i'm reaching the point
of it now being yet another name

our photos are beginning to mean nothing to me too,
your smile doesn't make my heart hurt anymore
and some days i don't think of you at all

but when i lay in bed
and i realize i made it through the day without picturing your smile
or hearing your laugh
a fear arises inside me —
because if i don't have the pain either
i don't have anything at all.

it's like i went back in time
to world before you existed
and something about that makes me feel empty.

i don't know how to let you go.

exist

it's easy to forget sometimes
that we're just here
to simply exist

there is no right or wrong
good or bad
loss or gain

we're here to exist;
live, breathe, be.

one day

if our chapter ever closes
i'll forever be praying
that it one day
reopens.

ghosts

you are no longer you
and somehow that changed me
because we are no longer us
we're just ghosts of what we used to be.

still here

things can escalate so quickly
feelings can grow
or resentment can arise
much like the push
or pull of a tide

it is easy here
to lose your way,
to do things you wouldn't normally do,
or speak words you wouldn't normally say

you can get caught up
lose sight of who you are
wander too deeply
and get too far

too far from you,
the you that is true
but it's okay, love,
you can always come back
your life will be waiting
for you to come home, too.

full circle

but i guess i should've known, right?

you can't have a powerful pull,
a connection that nearly sets your heart on fire,
without having an ending that does the same.

you can't have an authentic connection
you know, the kind that makes you believe in soulmates
without it blowing up in the same vibrancy it started with.

if your hearts are going to dance immensely,
there's going to be bloody hands when it ends;
there's going to be shattered dreams
broken hearts
and souls that no longer know their place in the world.

paris in the rain

i let my pain
wash down the drain
of these chaotic streets

i forgot who i was
and became who i wanted to be

there's nothing quite like
paris in the rain.

remain

what you took from me
i do not lack
because once i healed
i gained it all back.

how you heal

every rise and fall
every push and pull

you're allowed to feel
every emotion as you heal

do not bury them inside
do not wish your lungs be still,

you may not be okay now
but eventually you will.

seasons change,
so does love

and if i were the winter
you'd be a summer breeze
-- knowing that no matter the warmth --
you'll always come
and you'll always leave.

loneliness

peaceful
yet terrifying
your thoughts are your own
no matter how deep and dark they may go
---
but here, you see, you can be yourself
here, you can breathe.

the process

breathe it in
accept it
let it go.

hurricane

violent winds
full of vibrant sins
who would've thought
it would end like this.

pleasure

my stillness is enhanced
by the presence of yours

my heart is at home
when it's no longer mine

but it becomes ours.

let me go

you're holding onto me
because I'm the last bit of you
-the you that you want to be-
that you have

but this ended long ago
so please just let me go.

sunshine

the thing is
about a light like yours
is that others can make it brighter
but not a soul that walks this earth
can shadow its vibrancy.

and if there is one thing
i'd hope you could remember about yourself
it is that simple
and truest fact.

the smoke, it slides

the wind blew the snow
and it slid off the mountain side
like smoke
and i couldn't help but notice
that it looked like
the smoke that slips
through my mother's lips

why is something so beautiful
reminding me of such tragedy

i guess that's the thing about pain

it is sometimes beautiful
too.

the last time

and i've decided
that this is the last time

the last time my thoughts
are consumed by the shape of you

the last time the waves pull me under
and drown me in the depths of you

the last time i search for closure
in unanswered questions
and closed doors

this is the very last time
that i hold onto any debate
between holding on and letting you go

this is the last time i allow myself
to remember the feeling of you.

creativity

i enjoy the times that my creativity comes to life

when it boils through my veins
and gives my emotions
the voice that they've been fighting for

the fear subsides
and my freedom takes off
and i'm lost in the world
of my vibrant-self.

ocean

when i think of the deep blue
i think of you
the crashing of the waves
and the stillness of it too

i imagine your soul running free
like the birds up above
and your heart loving deeply
to the darkest depths of the sea

and sometimes i wish i was there
and that you'd still be with me.

stronger

your petty posts
and your low blows
they don't define me
not even close.

butterfly

damn you
for making me believe
as though my feelings are poisonous
that my love isn't worthy
and my heart is undeserving

for making me believe
that expressing myself
is unhealthy

for making me believe
that my anxiety is exaggerated
and my heartache is a problem

damn you
for making me believe
that questioning who i am
should be a constant

for making me believe
that if i were a butterfly
i have yet to bloom
and my home should permanently
be locked in this cocoon
that i will forever be
lacking light
in this darkness
that shadows my vibrancy

damn you
for making me believe
that i am any less than

so here's to you,
for i have finally bloomed.

unbreakable

i cannot control
your lack of belief in me

but i can control
what it does
or doesn't do to me.

a bigger world

i thought to myself:
"this is why you travel, this moment right here"

to feel this bliss
and contentment in the loneliness
the loneliness i've grown to value
as much as i hold affection from others

and this freedom
this genuine
overpowering
freedom
is something i can truly never feel at home
it is only on the road
that i can breathe this way

and i wonder if that is what i'll live for,
this freedom

or if i'll one day crave some steadiness.

your head

i wonder what goes through your head
when you think of me

is it the pain,
or is the love firmly planted in your memory?

i can tell you how it goes for me:
it's the pain at first
the tears,
the heartbreak,
the let down
and the wave of utter misery i still feel when i'm alone at night.

but somehow
in between the heartache that rushes in
your smile materializes in my mind
and my heart is filled with immense love,
causing me to remember why i loved you
all over again.
i remember the compassion
the love
the laughs
and your smile
my god,
your smile

and for awhile i remain there
in the stillness of these memories —
being captivated by the emotions that follow
wondering if your soul lights up
the way that mine does

when you think of me.

blossomed

your love runs through me
the way my creativity does

blossoming in unknown parts of my body
and beautifying every inch
that it vibrantly blooms.

tracing you

are you thinking of me
the way i'm thinking of you
because it seems as though
my thoughts are rather consumed

wrapped through the ins and outs
of every shade of you.

yesterday

yesterday
my niece wanted to swim in the ocean
but the waves were too big
and the tide was too strong
so i had to tell her no

she begged and begged
to swim just once

she could handle it,
she said
but i couldn't let her
with the chance of her drowning

and for the same reasons i tell her no
i tell myself
when it comes to you

because if i dive into you again
i will surely drown

and maybe you don't understand
the same way that she doesn't

but it's safer this way

because with you
i always end up gasping for air
when you pull me out of the shallows
and wrap me into you

and i'd rather live alone
than drown with you.

we're all lost

longer roads
empty homes
shattered glass
and absent stones

we're all a bit broken
and remembering that
makes me feel less alone.

sunflower

you are a sunflower
surrounded by snow

covered in nothing but black and white,
cold and pain
but there you stand
full of vibrant color and sunshine,
growing beautifully,
standing tall
---
you are a sunflower
surrounded by snow
being your own ray of sunshine
as you bloom and you grow.

better off

i notice the absence of you
but i notice the lack of heartache too

and i guess if i had to pick
whether to keep neither
or both

i'd choose to walk away from you.

waterfall

you crashed into my heart
the way the water does
hard and fast —
terrifying

but then calm and steady —
captivating

a love that lasts
as long as the riverbeds —
everchanging and everlasting.

trees

when you're lost
and you feel like you can't breathe
find a place to be alone
a little lost beneath the trees

remember that the sun will break
and you will too
because like the trees
you're allowed to be
exactly *you*.

self-care

i learned to nurture my emotional-health
the way i had been caring for yours

my life took a turn then
it felt like it was in my own hands again
or maybe even for the first time

what a powerful moment it was
for me to realize
that my heart deserved
all it had been giving to yours.

if you come back

if you come back
you should just know
i don't believe the way i used to
not in me
and not in you

though my forgiveness is in full bloom
as far as letting you back in
there is no room

if you come back, this time,
you should just know
i'll mean it
when i say no

because after all the pain
i learned to truly let you go.

the collector of things

the collector of things
i thought i could be

falling sort of in love with absolutely everyone,
loving what they couldn't see

the way their eyes dance when they smile
or the way they bite their lip when they listen to stories
that capture their presence

i collect only these parts of people,
their most vibrant pieces

i fall in love with someone
-something-
every day
collecting them as new parts of me.

no longer yours to take

i'm done giving pieces of myself
to you
because the truth is
is that i never get them back
and you seem to wander
so carelessly
with parts of me
on your sleeve.

lost in the clouds

do you ever watch the clouds move
wishing you could move across the earth
the way that they do

changing and adapting the way they do
being able to bring both light and darkness
rain and sunshine
the way that they do

and then remember
that we do?

that we, too, constantly move in the same
swift way they do
that we bring light
but can cloud it too
that we grow and reshape to those around us
and that just like the clouds
we can always move, grow,
change and shine
the way that they do

because yeah,
me too.

queen without a throne

and you'll think the world of her
because she could be

but you'll lose sight
of who she actually is

which is nowhere near
who she would be
if she was who you believed in.

you

your smile puts my heart at ease
it gives my pain a sense of relief
it feeds my soul a vibrant peace

your love,
it is a part of me.

the heartache subsides

one day

you'll let go of what is heavy

it won't be overnight
and it won't be as early
as you had hoped

but surely
the heaviness will subside
and you'll embrace the lightness
your heart has craved
and so righteously deserved
for so long.

beautiful beating heart

i realized
just on this exact day
that my heart still loves
the same way it still beats

and how incredible
is this heart of mine
that after it all
it chooses to shine.

emotional baggage

my shoulders ached
where your weight layed
the pounds of your
negative thoughts of me

and the guilt and shame
that you stacked along my vertebrae

so i started unpacking
and leaving the thoughts of you behind

the load was so much lighter,
allowing me to walk
(to grow)
so much further.

whole

your scars
however deep they may go
still haven't scratched
even the surface of your soul.

you're still bright, my love,
you're still whole.

my own light

it feels so hard to decide
whether i can exist in a life without you
when i've been so used to one with you

but i finally realized
there's a world that lives
vibrantly
without either

because life isn't white
nor black without you
there's an entire light between
that is unphased
by you being
or not being in my life

my life is not defined
by the presence of yours.

uncertainty

no matter how pure the love
how steady the job
how strong the life,
a healthy level of uncertainty
will always remain

but do not let this fact
hold you to hesitation and fear
there is something to be loved
in the truth of uncertainty

it is that we too
are allowed to be uncertain
and free.

in bloom

let your tears fall
into the soil of your soul
letting your pain go
and your passion grow

let your heart break
as you drop to your knees
allowing your pain
to do nothing but release

paint over your soil
with vibrant emotion
breathe it in
soak it up
and watch it dissipate

you're no longer a you that you once knew
but the new, brighter you, is here in full bloom.

thank you for reading my words; these pages are filled with parts of me that can sometimes be scary to share. i wanted to end this book with a message to you, with affirmations i hope you read aloud on days you need it. we all need it sometimes.

xxx,
brynn

daily affirmation 1:

love lives inside of me
and it is stronger
than any form of doubt
or lack of self-worth.

daily affirmation 2:

i deserve the purest love,
the most genuine compassion,
and true, absolute kindness.

i will not settle for less.

daily affirmation 3:

i am capable of maintaining tough skin
along with a gentle heart

flowing freely with love
and a healthy level of skepticism.

daily affirmation 4:

i am capable
of remaining enthusiastic
and compassionate
no matter what the circumstances may be.

daily affirmation 5:

self-care and personal growth
will always remain a top priority in my life
even through hardships
because that is what i deserve.

daily affirmation 6:

i believe in myself wholeheartedly.
self-doubt will not make a home of me.
i am strong and i am capable.

daily affirmation 7:

i am capable and deserving
of dissecting my thoughts and feelings
in a more understanding and less-anxious, judgy way.

daily affirmation 8:

i will work on being the "me"
that i want to be
because i deserve that, and i believe in it.

daily affirmation 9:

i deserve the same compassion
that i show to my loved ones.

daily affirmation 10:

i will always find it within myself
to stay hopeful during the lows
and humble and inspired during the highs.
i can love myself throughout them both.

afterword

mental health can be a tricky thing. it's hard to understand how we as humans can feel so much joy, and somehow, in the same 48hrs, feel pain that seems to stem from our core. this book is filled with pages of the ins and outs of these feelings. most of these were written in a very vulnerable state, and i didn't think they would ever be shared with the world like they are now, but i decided to do so in hopes that they connect with you somehow and help you heal in some way. about half of these poems were written about, or inspired by the feelings of, my closest friends and their stories as well; completely driven by empathy and the words i wanted to say to them but couldn't find how. that being said, these pages were written for you, too. assuming you've felt the same pain, heartache, love, and passion that me and the people in my life have felt. you are not alone in the waves of emotions you feel. i hope these pages remind you of that. i hope you can refer back to the words that sparked something in you when you need to hear them again. thank you for reading my words.
and a very special thank you to my friends and family that helped me not only put this book together, but inspired some of my favorite poems within it. super extra very special thank you to my grandma and grandpa, and their best friends Les and Steven, for letting me hide out at their lake house for weeks to finish this book.
i love you all, so much.

xxx,
brynn

*we're all covered
in our own vibrant colors.*

Made in the USA
Las Vegas, NV
08 August 2021